8 Butterfly Questions

for Gardening

by Heidi Ferris

Other Growing Green Hearts books in this series:
- 1-2-3 Earth, Air & Me
- Your 4 S's: Senses, Sun, Systems, Seasons
- 5 R's: Rethink, Reduce, Reuse, Recycle, Rejoice*
- 6 C's: Creation, Christ, Creativity, Combustion, Climate, Connect*
- 7 Water Wonderings
- 8 Butterfly Questions

Books that include science and faith together.

www.growinggreenhearts.com

Growing Green Hearts

About This Series

This series of books, Playing with Science and Systems, has been created to be simple, scientifically accurate, and sometimes focused on faith. Science is problem finding and problem solving. The author Heidi Ferris is passionate about encouraging youth to ask questions, boosting science literacy, empowering kids to care for our shared resources, and exploring the wonders in God's creation. Heidi lives in Minnesota with her family - not far from the Mississippi River.

—

This book is dedicated to the Eleanors of both past and present who reach out to the world with love and leadership.

Copyright © 2016 Heidi Ferris, Growing Green Hearts LLC
Written and Edited by: Heidi Ferris
Graphic Design: Lisa Carlson, Spiira Design
Series Consultant: Janine Hanson, Janine Hanson Communications
A special note about photo credits:
    Willem (age 13) took the pictures on pages 3 and back cover
    Eleanor (age 7) took the pictures on pages 16 (large), 16 (small), and 22 (large)

All rights reserved. No part of this publication may be reproduced, stored in a retrieval system, or transmitted in any form or by any means, electronic, mechanical, photocopying, recording, or otherwise, without prior permission. For information regarding permission contact Growing Green Hearts LLC.

Contents

8 Butterfly Questions

1. Who has seen a butterfly land on a flower?.. 6
2. What do butterflies need?... 8
3. Do caterpillars and butterflies eat the same things for dinner?................. 10
4. How long does it take for a caterpillar to change into a butterfly?............ 11
5. Why is prairie land important?.. 12
6. What's happening underneath a butterfly garden?................................... 14
7. How can children start a garden for butterflies?...................................... 16
8. Which is more important - clean water, plants, animals, or clean air?....... 22
Glossary 24

1

Who has seen a butterfly land on a flower?

You can find butterflies on colorful prairie flowers. A butterfly garden is filled with plants that butterflies like the best.

② What do butterflies need?

Butterflies need the correct temperature, food, water, air, sunshine, hiding spots and rest.

8

This picture shows swallowtail butterflies drinking nectar from purple cone flowers.

Do caterpillars and butterflies eat the same things for dinner?

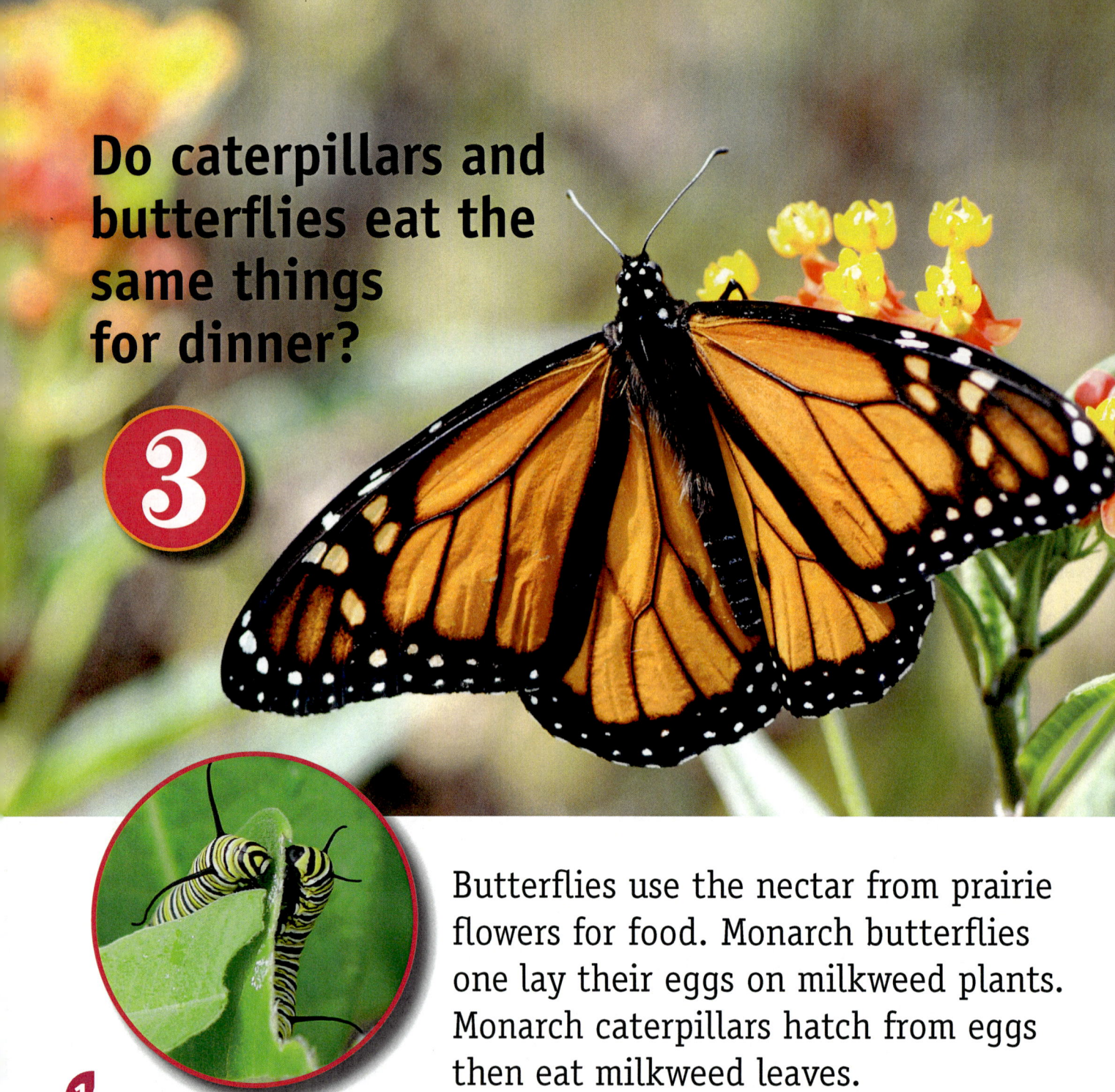

Butterflies use the nectar from prairie flowers for food. Monarch butterflies one lay their eggs on milkweed plants. Monarch caterpillars hatch from eggs then eat milkweed leaves.

How long does it take for a caterpillar to change into a butterfly?

These swallowtail caterpillars are eating the leaves from a dill plant. Once big enough, usually 2 weeks, each caterpillar will curl into a "J" shape under a leaf, split its skin to reveal a chrysalis, then change into a butterfly after about 10 days.

5

Why is prairie land important?

Prairie plants help butterflies, feed birds, and clean our shared air and water.

Who lives here? What do they eat?

6 What's happening underneath a butterfly garden?

The roots of prairie flowers and grasses can be over 10 feet deep! The roots hold soil in place and that helps keep our rivers and lakes clean. The roots get bigger and deeper when the plant above ground uses air, sunlight, and water to grow.

7

How can children start a garden for butterflies?

It is best to give prairie flowers and grasses a head start. Do this by starting seeds inside in late winter.

Seeds can be purchased at a garden store or collected from prairie plants.

Tools you will need are seeds, trays, soil mix, trays with lids and a lamp.

Your wet starter mix should be at least 1 inch deep. Plant seeds then cover the trays to trap heat. Use a lamp with timer to give the seeds 12 hours of light a day.

Seedlings can be planted outside once they have leaves and the the soil has warmed.

 **Which is more important: clean water, plants, animals, or clean air?**

They are all important! Water, air, earth, and living things on this planet are all connected.

23

Glossary

Water cycle:	Water moving around our planet as a liquid, solid, and gas
Butterfly Garden:	A collection of plants that meet the needs of butterflies
Prairie:	A large area of grassland shaped by rolling hills or flat land
Nectar:	The sweet liquid made by plants; food for butterflies
Chrysalis:	The hard case that protects the caterpillar turning into a butterfly
Seedling:	A young plant growing forth from the seed

Made in the USA
Middletown, DE
07 February 2016